If Nothing

If Nothing

MATTHEW NIENOW

Alice James Books

NEW GLOUCESTER, MAINE

alicejamesbooks.org

10 9 8 7 6 5 4 3 2 1

Alice James Books are published by Alice James Poetry Cooperative, Inc.

Alice James Books
Auburn Hall
60 Pineland Drive, Suite 206
New Gloucester, ME 04260
www.alicejamesbooks.org

Library of Congress Cataloging-in-Publication Data

Names: Nienow, Matthew, author.
Title: If nothing / Matthew Nienow.
Description: New Gloucester, Maine : Alice James Books, 2025.
Identifiers: LCCN 2024033505 (print) | LCCN 2024033506 (ebook) | ISBN
    9781949944693 (trade paperback) | ISBN 9781949944419 (epub)
Subjects: LCGFT: Poetry.
Classification: LCC PS3614.I368 I36 2025 (print) | LCC PS3614.I368
    (ebook) | DDC 811/.6--dc23/eng/20240722
LC record available at https://lccn.loc.gov/2024033505
LC ebook record available at https://lccn.loc.gov/2024033506

Alice James Books gratefully acknowledges support from individual donors, private foundations, the
National Endowment for the Arts, and the Poetry Foundation (https://www.poetryfoundation.org).

Cover photo provided by author.

CONTENTS

∞

For Elie, and the chance to be new—

Inside us there is something that has no name, that something is what we are.

—JOSÉ SARAMAGO

ON THE CONDITION OF BEING BORN

As you were, then. As you were
at the moment of your first breath
outside the mother, good
before you knew any other way to be.
Who can remember such a time?
I rely on photographs to ply memory,
the first son, cut out of my wife, the second,
pushed straight into my hands
in the back room of our small rented house.
Both bearing the same unowned
goodness, bright as a noon sun
in summer. It hurt to look straight at it
and stayed in the eye like a wound
the brain was trying to understand or undo.
Maybe it lasted an hour. Maybe three
days or three weeks. I don't know
that it is the same in every case, but what if
being human didn't mean that we had to
fuck this up? I've been wanting
to ask questions there are no answers to,
the kind that might elicit only a *hmmm*
in response, or a hymn in some cases,
as though song could shed light
upon such inquiry. Maybe if it was
a wordless hymn, the melody could
reach back into what held us before
we were broken into different lines.
Source. As in, the mother's mother.
Doesn't it feel good to lie on the earth?
I mean, actually lie down in your day clothes,
face against some grass, to just lie there
and for a moment stop pretending you are
separate from it, to stop pretending you didn't
come from it and won't go back, eyes open

or closed, thinking or not, the negative charge
of the very ground taking up all the excess
voltage you didn't even know you had.

EVERY GIFT CARRIES A COST

It is difficult to go back
into the burning
into the bitter bowl
the knife
my grandfather gave me
carving char & resin
its plastic scales
meant to approximate
bone   my grandfather
now only ash & shards
of bone in a bag
in a brown cardstock
cylinder no bigger
than my fist   bound
with twine   I can't
look at him as I use
his knife   as I smudge
the silver glint
against the heated
glass aching for
a chemical dose
of what I think must
at the cellular level
approximate the bodily
feeling of love

USELESS PRAYER

After the night & its empty bottles, Lord, brown glass
in a paper bag, the music of breaking

like the voices of angels, un-
intelligible, I fold my hands together in the sign

of prayer & begin, *O Lord of How-Time-Flies,*
swatting days down from the calendar, each

drawn like a cell & with bars to keep
who's boss known, Lord of the sour stomach

& slow walk to the grease-joint burger stand
to get a dose of dopamine, my brain in sync

with the flickering fluorescents in the gas station
coolers, the beer just below room temp—

O Lord of my last dollar, I need a longer drink.
I'd close my eyes for good, Lord,

but someone has been tampering with the dark

WHAT LUCK

I lived. Lived again. Wrecked,
hungover. Swerved in the dark
from river back to bunk
and never hit a tree. Never was
pulled over when my only
tongue was *Swamp*. Locked
my keys in the trunk in a thunder
storm, done hotboxing the Cimarron
with can't remember, car halfway
in the road. Aura of blunt, pungent
as roadkill skunk. Always made it
home. Always stumbling thick-
tongued, lucky if I didn't get the spins,
mumbling if I had to speak, numb
thing dumb in the truest sense.
Floor was floor and I was on it, gone
wind in a way. Also stone.
Somehow sang even undone.
Almost alone, even throned
among future tombs, I lived,
the coal of my heart on a slow
burn, no time to lose, no such
thing as time, eyes tuned
to the lack of light, skull
locked tight, crowned alive, the King
of Lost Keys.

BEGINNER'S MIND

I was the Midas

of pain, holding a knife

in each hand. It was

the only thing that felt

right. I kicked the dog.

Screamed at my sons.

Broke every promise

I'd made. I do not

deserve this

chance to be good.

DUSK LOOP

Some things, then, cannot be repaired and must go on, into a kind of dusk
that seems somehow endless, somehow stuck on a short loop, the way
high-minded thieves trick security guards before breaking into the vault,
switching over the live feed of a camera to a prerecorded scene in which
nothing happens. And because we have seen this done so many times now
in that same repeated movie, we can believe it really happens, and because
we can believe it, it must be so. A master hand hits a switch at a well-timed
blink and, voila, a dusk that is always that same dusk rolls on, the backdrop
to all the memories I can still access in which I was terrible to you, my
dear boy, all the times I raged at your sweet, how it was me that eventually
broke it free from your small hands and did not stop it from drifting away.
Because the dusk keeps being that same dusk, I don't have to change. I am
always performing some act of cruelty, always hearing your confused, sad cry
when I said your mother and I were splitting up. I held you too close then.
What could you need from me now? No apology will ever be enough.

IN DEED

So much for words, then.
So much for the silent

figure of a father held
in the arms of a padded rocker.

Forget your blanket of wants.
Forget the list of your longing.

A pencil is a fine weapon
if you know how to hold it.

This world expects a man
to prove that he exists.

The contract you signed
at birth clearly stated loaves

are expected of you. Bring them.
Earn your share of love.

I WAS ALMOST ALWAYS UNDER

the heavy thumb of that

amber stranger

whose hands I kissed

in trance

        who I followed

lemming-like   over

every ledge

        until falling

was my finest form

IN THE MIRROR LOOKING BACK

like an old man though I was
barely thirty   bloated & sad
unless in the early stages
of each day's first drink
so actively helpless
I made it impossible
for honesty to exist
all story   all pointless
& probably essential
to who I have become
for I can now see beyond
the day   & have enrolled
in forgiveness studies   I am
making nice with the road
(pardon this lapse
into solipsism
a moth just now
winked at me
its brilliant wings
patterned like eyes)

DAILY LOG #104

Drunk again. One tall bottle of that monk brew Golden
Monkey and a sixer of Rainier that went down like water.
Lights off in the shop, hoping no one comes to the door.
YouTube disaster marathon, especially tsunamis. I take breaks
to piss and look out over my tools, feel the briefest desire
to build before a wall of to-dos rises in steady pace.
The dog wants to play, and I could use a toke but don't
want to be seen, so I slip out back and keep her close.
This place is a tomb for dreams I've been claiming as my own.

BOOKENDING THE DAY

A simple mind would call it bud and pack a bowl and toke
just out of bed, but I know better having lived to toke

between my many tasks. I found wax more suitable for subtlety
and could fit one in before sitting in the Legos, another toke

before the drive and after dropping the kids at school. I'd repack
the pen and at the press of a button, I was holding in my lungs a toke

so sweet and pungent I couldn't help but cough my way into a kind of bliss.
At the shop I feigned sharpness at the blade and went out back to toke

and toss the ball for the dog, the luminous pressure behind my eyes
glossing over gray. Winter was no match for what could burn, and toke

I did through all the darkest days. I was stoned so much that great quantities
of concentrate could barely dull my concentration and the more I toked

the more I needed to toke in order to be granted leave
of what existential doubt I could not yet explain. I existed, a token

of a man, at surface seeming all in and swimming with the best of them,
but inside I felt bested at a game of my own invention and missing a toke

would mean a knife was in my hand, my intentions blurred, but visible:
I wouldn't live another day in this body, but I wouldn't leave my sons, and so toked,

my breath bated, my own snare set with purest bait. Please don't say my name,
Green God, or otherwise appease me. I've turned over a new leaf. No toke can free me.

DEEPWELL TRAVERSE

With amber in the mouth
      I treaded emptiness

drew in clouds of dank and never
seemed to fill
            I could not
mute the single droning note

dimming light with doubt
and a crushing want   so bad

I could not go a day without
thinking of   very specifically   how

to kill myself and that I should
my god   how deep that well

seemed to be   how
pointless its depth
            and so

I walked straight into the fire and took
my place amongst the ash

COCOON

After years of binge   my hunger
was suddenly gone

I became still
for three whole minutes

during which a curt north wind
dusted my sills with a memory of ice

Everything changed then

I put aside my sickle and walked from the field
though the day was young

and found a shade in which to begin

I did not think about the task
beyond that it felt   when noticed   like nothing

more than breathing
I began with nothing

to show and soon a veil of fibers around my feet
and soon a quilt that felt like knowing

how to dance and dancing well
and so I spun   for what else

was there to do
I no longer went out   I didn't know how to be

a friend or father   I didn't
know what a lover was   I stopped

pretending the world was to blame

I was inside with no story
to save me from myself

AT MIDLIFE TRYING TO RECALL MY TWENTIES

You ever feel like your soul is twisted
up in a funny knot you don't remember
tying? Some shit must have gone down
while you were blacked out & moving
about the world, some lowly worming,
likely: i.e. inching closer to any
interesting woman just to see if you might
be lure enough to light the want in her eyes,
i.e. practicing your subtle magic & then
going about another day as if nothing
happened. Uncork some spirits &
collaborate. Smooth out some of the kinks
in your heartsleeve. Unravel if you must.
Daylight is another world & for now
the night is doing you all kinds of favors.
Lick a cheek & go wild, you godless scrap.
Mount the escarpment for a better view.
Forget the why of the ascent & cling
with your life to the smallest holds. Don't
ever downclimb. Don't you dare
give regret an inch, even if that
scramble to the edge almost kills you.

EARLY ONSET

Your deeds should follow your word. Addiction
is a full-time job. I am house broken and have broken
the horse. I am morse code on opposite day. The hole
I punched in the wall is how I feel. I am a place
for mice to enter. The mold on the bathroom sill
is my middle name. Under a microscope I am
iridescent. I am a we and our story is soon
to be a major motion picture. The new world
is all screen, cracked or no, grease smear or gleam.
From chaos the mind makes order. A narrative.
A self narrates. I was the bad one in the bunch.
I almost rotted the rest with my needs. Little red
stars dot the white walls where I slapped
mosquitoes while reading each night in bed.

IN THE LANGUAGE OF MY KIN

Put me in a room
with the well-heeled,

with the fast-talking

intellects & I
am a Mylar balloon

deflating. I don't

have the quote
of the century

for each point

I make. Can't call up
from the dead

another's eloquence

to support my thought.
I am shovel-born,

calloused hands

working the knots
from a woman's

shoulders. Her sighs

are the only
currency I consider.

I drink gallons of water

by day & piss
outside under

a veranda of stars.

The wind is my cousin.
Broken branches

my once removed.

RAISON D'ÊTRE: NIGHT WORK

To dig in the dark for night sounds
To sniff at the earth caught under fingernails
To wonder at what grows in the turnover

of freshly mulched mounds   feasting on the rot
the fists of windfall apples opening

green strawberries half eaten by rats
raspberry stalks and plum pits
To feel heat rising from the compost and know

I have wasted so many days

AFTER THE FIRE

It wasn't a total loss,
for out of the earth rose
bright kernels of light—
pinks and blues, luminescent
against the charred dirt,
against the ash of what
had lived in one form
and now, through
a particle exchange,
would be house, would
be bread, and word,
would be lust and nerve,
soft machines intelligent
in many kinds of hope—
nothing lost, actually,
nothing ever actually lost
in the borderless realm
of time and the shapes
that case the misplaced
energy of the stars.

SOMETIME IN MARCH 2017

I finished the bottle.

Held a knife to my chest.

Swayed in the wind, shirtless

among cedars. A globe

of blood at the tip

of the blade. I faced

away from the house,

though no one was home.

The thought was a leap

from a ledge or a long

swim too far from shore

to make the return.

I can't say why

I hesitated. I was

this close

to erasing my name.

IN ALL THE WRONG PLACES

Some days, it seemed happiness came before
the bottle, arriving at dawn or noon,
some bland scene I'd be walking through
suddenly smiling at the light hitting the leaves
of one tree across the way & effortlessly
I would be, for a moment, the tree
burning in the lumens of our star—
but of course, I had to work & being my own boss
meant that time was like math in 11th grade—
I didn't get it & stared dumbly at the teacher
who repeated the word *arbitrary* so often
I almost grasped what it meant, though
I'll admit there was a part of me that thought
of tributaries when he spoke & I'd be gone
again, wading upstream, usually between
steep banks with the sound washing over me
like a thousand distant conversations, & I
preferred it this way, being outside
of earshot, thirsty for wonder, unable
to quench or quell the ache of it always ending
just as it was getting good.

FOUR YEARS TO THE DAY

but I am still crushed
by that old devotion to drink

to the dream of bitter floral notes
of hops in iced cups on repeat

the swoon of a binge
my daily homage

to the excess of nature
the overkill of spring

my immaculate tongue always
ready to indulge

the deluge of a want
I mislabeled *need*

even though years pass
in which I bow & bow

to nothing   nothing
bows back

THEY ONCE LOOKED TO ME

to know the world.
I gave them words

as tenderly as I could
in my boozy breath,

a bottle always in my hand—
they wanted to be near,

to build alongside me,
back when I still

believed anything
was possible, before I tried

my hand at making a house
only to see it crumble

under daily use. My sons,
they used to see me

as something fully formed
even in the days when

I would only wake to pack
a bowl & toke. Once,

they looked to me
to know how to feel

about the world. If
only I could erase

the memory of their eyes
when they finally understood.

ON THE OTHER SIDE

Do you really want to know
what it was like

on the inside of my hunger?

For what it is worth, in every
room of our little house, the evidence

of their vibrancy, my knowledge

of their need—it saved me
from myself. If there is a window

that opens at night, who

visits me is not for you to know.
Though I may lead you to believe

I have done this alone, feathers

litter the sill. Had I been
childless, nothing

would have called me from the edge.

INTEREST OWED

I forget, sometimes,
when the hammer

is in my hand
and my shirt

is soaked through,
or when I am

digging deep
into the earth

for a reason
that will keep

the lights on,
alive in my

purpose, vibrant
to the bone,

some debts
take more than

one lifetime
to pay down.

FOR EVERY PART THAT SHOWS

I will sing in my quietest
to that which does not:

For every hidden
For every kept swell of joy or
For every line in the mind that's true & you & you alone

For what is remaindered from the shards of
For what is stored to feed need's invention
For the plainly-named secret another deposits in your care

For the bruise & if you love what gave it to you
For the very place where

For the sake of
For the sake of
    & even why it seemed okay at the time*

For what should not have been but is to never go away

For how you do
    & maybe even how you learned to do

For what has no voice of its own & is not asking to be spoken for

For what has no need to be said

For if you do
    & what will happen then
    & if a god can already see, or a woman

---

* (...to lay all day on the remote coast in the sun unburdened / of my clothes & lifelong timidity with the body I was given, / alongside her in the sand, not touching but / there together & when she ran into the sea at dusk / a buoyant laughter in the shape of her body / as it exuberantly was—)

For what other reason to have a mind that can sift what passes through & before oneself—
that oneself is found & made in the sifting!

> To give this away?
> To just give this away? This whole

For what lives in you best quietly
no matter how sweet the song of sharing

I bow down into myself
It must be so

IT COULD HAVE BEEN OTHERWISE

is a truly useless thing to say   unless

you are once again standing in the same

moment about to say yes

to the woman who has come to you

in a gauze of hesitation

but who arrived without

any underwear below her skirt

her decision already made

at least regarding fucking in the grass

to the metronome of desire

a faint ticking above the buzz of summer

wearing the face she learned watching movies

the way most of us learned

what fucking could be like

but most often is not

Sometimes we get it right

if only for a brief interval and find

ourselves in the dream we have seen

on some screen somewhere in the unmarked

past   the pages of our own

history neatly edited   carefully curated

to keep intact a story of exactly who

we are and how we came to be

For too much of my life I turned away

as the brightest moments reached

their peak so as to be in the ache

of the ripe skin   the body ready

to burst with sweetness

I must have been afraid (I was afraid)

of the silent downturn after

any climax and tried to build

a house of memory from the nearly

perfect and always impermanent scenes

a new favorite song on repeat   tugging

at the want in me to be   for a moment

enough to risk everything for   I tried

to build a whole life of such ephemera

and each time failed   yes   it could

have been otherwise   and yet I wear this face

as though I have no idea how much it hurts you

I KISS THE GROUND WHERE WE LAY

but curse the reckless *yes*

in long June grass

where we   in sweet air

like snakes in slow need

played patient

only in that we did not

run at each other

only in that we let lips

& tongues undo years

for a taste of salt   of honey

slow as the honey

combing our hive   our wings

wet with captured light   our

hum humming the only

the only   the *yes*

for all yeses

the *please* of more

open mouths meeting

in green noon   our brief

hunger   no kin

to consequence

REGRET

It used to have me
on a lead   that remorse

but I learned to ride it

that dear horse upon whose
flanks I have grown

into a man who owns

his work and no longer
hides in drink or smoke

BEGIN AGAIN

And for what? To say that we did our best? To say *I really am sorry* and believe
it will translate into anything meaningful to our children,

as though they could pardon us, could gently guide us to take a knee,

lifting our chins as spines of sunlight poke around their faces, making
it impossible to see anything specific about their features, so that they might be

anyone, really, a figure from a painting by someone long dead who never dreamed

of saying anything this important—and so the words hang in the air, indiscernible,
like a conversation heard through a wall, all tone and inflection, more hum than hymn—

as if we had forgotten all we had learned, that there is no going back,
no erasing the past, only going forward, slightly stooped

with the weight of memory, somehow heavier with its impression, watching
the slow replay of betrayal. Of course there is no going back. If we're to continue

living we must eventually walk through the fires we've built, unless we want to strand
ourselves on the far side, where no one can save us. The thing about this going forward

is that you must bear the burning, your skin taken right off, so that even the smallest wind

is a knife, even the breath of a lover, or a child, will tear at you, for a time, at least.
It took me almost forty years to face my father as an equal, to see his eyes

and understand what lives quietly in them. I must also have a realm

within me in which I weather the seasons, slowly paying back with interest
my debts, working to mend the wounds I caused, offering myself to accountability,

revealing my whole self to my wife and my children as as I show them with my life the painting of a figure walking through and beyond a field of flames—doing the work to own a portion of the pain, a serving to consume or be consumed by.

I mean to stand up now. Come at me, if you want. I'm more ready than I've ever been. Tell me what you long to say. I won't be angry. I'll listen. I'm listening now.

IT COULD BE THAT MY HEART WAS NOT IN IT

When winter crosses over the field & ten

thousand shards of ice trap a glint of dawn

in their shields, I cannot

say I would have rather made a life

from money, hiring the house built

while long hours away earned a wealth

our country says I should want.

Curator of the Intangible, Little Thief

of Whispers Hiding in Plain Sight

are names I give myself. I pay

attention to everything. What is it called

when the cure lives within the curse?

MAKE NO MISTAKE

See how far you get on goodness alone.
Make no mistake & the soul

has a hard time stretching out. It stays young

too long & aches in any leaning.
Lean out, then. Fuck up

in the most beautiful way possible—

every error a mirror
revealing something you may have been

unwilling to see

just before you took that chance
on the pigeon ledge, wanting to understand

the ubiquity of such birds.

HISTORY

There is no way I can explain the past
in a manner that doesn't somehow
free the sparrow from the barn,
but not before it crashes against the glass
over and over, falling to the bench. Stunned
and on its back, I scooped the sparrow
from the wood and carried it outside
while it slowly turned its head
and nipped my fingers with its beak,
a dun ghost weightless in my hands.
I gave the bird to the crook of a willow
then stood back. Even that day, I had
been thinking of killing myself. When
the bird finally flew, I was offered
no thanks, no revelation. Saving that
small life from the trap of a building
did not change me. At least not then,
when I could see no other way to be.
When it would have been impossible
for me to imagine ever being the bird.

AN ECHO FOR THE ARCHIVES

If nothing more
ever comes between us
I've chosen to remember
the white dress in June,
the long wait for a good meal
measured in the time it took
to sip two Moscow mules
in dimpled copper cups.
The server called us beautiful,
said we looked so very happy,
and we were, I believe. Truly so.
For the longer I dig in the dusky
tidelands of this human life,
I have found *happiness* to be
the most elusive of all states.
Yet, I can abide the right
to pursue a life more soulful
than industrious. It seems
the most human decree, in fact,
to champion the chase of such
momentary pleasure as
dining with a lover who
looks you in the eye with pure
acceptance of your flaws,
who seems to see them
and not care that they are large,
who wants you anyway for all
the good that glows beyond
your sin—who knows, even
then, before your order is taken
down, (as a dumb hope dulls
the mind) that it cannot
last, this youthful errand,
however canny in its aim.

How brief such a moment
may be before it rattles out,
echoing madly in mis-
remembered eternity.

GETTING OFF ANTIDEPRESSANTS

I remember back in withdrawal when I'd ghost
throughout the day. It was always a quick turn
of my head to the left or right and my body
would evaporate. Time broke free for however
long it took to become the ether and know it was
ether I had become. Then the slow fade back into
the realm we call life, where I was trying to decide
what to cook my kids for dinner. This went on
for weeks, while in my dreams a crystal vision
mapped out every meaningful encounter I'd had
with another soul. All those years packed into
brief nights I'd wake drenched in sweat,
more alive, it seemed, than I'd ever been, having,
in the dreams, worked to mend all the hurts
I'd caused, all the missed chances to be real,
to be on purpose in my deeds. And even
in the dreams I often left unforgiven,
but I had tried and knew I was enough, that
the road ahead of me would be soft and thistle-
laden, that I would have to feel the spines
needling at my feet, but that I could also choose
to be warmed by the purple torches they offered up.

SEAMS OF STARLIGHT & FLECKS OF GOLD

There is a realm

within the body

where the soul resides,

a speck of starlight.

The soul is borrowed

& does not thrive

without a bit of pain

to work against.

But only a fool

seeks out suffering.

It will find you,

cracking the glass,

sowing doubt

in every field.

It will find you,

& you may choose

to let it in. If you can

live with loss, the soul

grows bright.

Like the sun,

it touches everything.

OWNERSHIP

Guilt's my godfather,
footing all the bills.
Cleaning out my chimney
each spring, bags and bags
of ash. I know how good
I have it. I know.
Don't need you telling me
every time you come by
marveling in the splendor
of this small paradise.
The deed is in our name.
That ludicrous paper
the assessor updates
each year, splitting house
and land. Owls, tree frogs.
Ravens and robins. Slugs.
And rats. Acres of
cedar, fir, madrone, hemlock.
Coyotes in the valley
named for the sky.

THE RETURN

Here I am again,
staring out the window,

watching nothing
in particular happen

to the trees. I hear
a raven make

from nothing
a sound like a drop

of water—that
sound falling

into the cavern
of my brain.

How does one aim
toward nothing

without tripping
into nihilism?

I banished the drink
in order to live.

I returned
to myself

by making room
for nothing.

EVEN IF THE PAST IS NOT A PLACE YOU CAN VISIT

I sleep alone
if I sleep at all

climbing a rickety ladder
that claps against the rim

of the loft & hurts my feet
my bed just below the roof

where bamboo brushes
the metal snare of the corrugated

sheets   where willows knock
at the cedar siding & owls

call out voles from mounds
of twigs & leaves

I can wave to my wife
through a narrow window

before she turns out
the light in the bedroom

we used to share
back when sleep was somehow

less precious   back when
I still drank myself into

a heaviness & did not
roll restlessly through my past

waking with bruised
knees from my constant

kneeling   & even still
I do not forgive myself

FIVE YEARS NOW

without a drink, but in dreams
such timelines do not

exist. I can be 12 again, or 20.
I can be in the middle of hurting

myself for the final time,
in the middle of waking up

to whatever wounding meant
to that man almost gone

from every world I've known.
The ghost exists, then,

to reinforce apology. I see
a trace of his blue, and fold.

ALTERNATE ENDINGS

Sunbloom glaze on the hill almost
beautiful before we knew
our house was on fire.

o

Blended family. Shaved head, heavy
with the drink I never quit.

o

Viviendo en México con la novia
y sus abuelos, hablando mas
de la guerra que la paz.

o

On the street, fighting four coats
for warmth, pulling a box of half-
smoked cigarette butts collected
downtown.

o

Major in money and a house
to prove it. Trophy life glinting
like a wound.

APOLOGIA

Whoever said stone is unfeeling
does not know the measure of all feeling.

Channeling stone can save those who
would float away into realms of grief.

Holding against the storm,
I sit with my wife as she sobs.

I am, with my life,
carving my apology from this stone.

NO PAINTING WORTH ITS PAINT

If we could dream him back / we would.
— JOSH KALSCHEUR

But there is no going back, no way
to remove the memories of having lived

in that time, no way to undress the wound
and watch the blood run back

into the body, the jagged star closing
in on itself. Every sweetness must

eventually take its turn in the compost,
giving back the essence of its light. No

freeze-frame in the live world. No painting
worth its paint that does not somehow

move in the mind or reveal traces of the hand
that made it. All the second chances,

what did they teach me, if not to dream
more wildly toward a kingdom in which the king

was not so cruel? If I could be anyone
in the whole world, I would still be me.

It has taken me half a life to learn what love is
and is not. It has taken all the loss I could earn.

I ALMOST FORGET

It could be yesterday
I was standing in the yard

with three joints, folding
my hands over them

in a kind of prayer,
lighting one

after another to toke
deeply as I paced.

I remember that day
because it was my last.

And though I love
stories, I am not

the one I told
about need and loss.

I set that story down
to begin this living.

It was like returning
to myself after more

than twenty years away.
That day, I walked the field

to the forest path
aching for the change

and because of it. I didn't
know you had already

made peace with the idea
of leaving me, of loving me

from afar. What changed then,
when I told you I was done

for good? I was still stoned
when I made that claim, still

numb and unreachable
on that distant shore.

ODE TO ADD

Under the pile of coats

left at the base of the stairs

is a book I will never read.

I stare at it and dream

and never look beyond

the cover. I don't know why

I care so much about the costs

of distraction. Beauty

is a dream that ends well.

I am not my doings. Not

even my stillness. There is

a little glow that makes a sound

only children and the very old

can hear. It belongs to no one

and is in every animation.

Not animal. That is the body.

This is the token that makes it run.

That thing we call *joy*

that rises from the running.

MY DISORDER

&, sure, the dream is lavish & wears desire
coyly—who wouldn't allow their gaze

to follow blandly along the ghost trace

of a path through trees where wild
fruits catch the sun in the taut curves

of their skin?—O, to be a bird that could

easily bob through branches & settle
at the eating before dipping away

to another lure—but dreams are overrated,

unless your dream is the song
of *what was I saying?* O, winter sun

warm upon my face! I'll sing then,

even in damning the bills. Sing
even to the lingering sense of failure

reddening my mask of shame.

PASTORAL

Today I swam across
a little pond with my
eyes alone, slipping
through the barbed
wire fence that cuts it
clean in two, violent
reds and yellows of
another ending in which
I try to instill wonder
in my sons, marveling
aloud about beauty
and luck. They humor
me, but won't for long.
They must go off into
the labyrinth and find
the underwater entrance
blocked by the bones
of those who lacked
the verve and never
found, or were forced
into, that green glen
of ongoing gratitude.

LETTER OF RECOMMENDATION

I am writing on behalf of the wind in my son's hair,
which, at least in this photograph, is always there for him,
always cooling his cheeks and suggesting new scents
from over yon dale, you know the one, just out
of sight from the cidery yard where his friends run
with him into the alchemical twilight, which clothes
every living thing in the ephemeral silk of youth,
which is only enhanced by the wind that carries downy
seedpods and pollen, giving the light something to shine
through, and the wind does this all thanklessly, so humble,
remaining mostly unseen, bowing down low in the grasses,
sometimes precisely in one branch alone, more often
broadly present, bearing the soft, steady answer
to the long question of what it means to be free.

IF YOU THINK YOU KNOW THE WAY

the path confounds you
as a field of furrowed runs spreads out

in every direction, deep channels

of matted grass newly freed
from the overbearing weight of ice

and snow, at least where the sun

is free to traverse the valley. A bit further
on, you're still postholing thigh-deep

in crusty pack, no matter that it's May.

Whatever trail might lie below the snow
is for another year. You can guess

your way along the creek, calling *hey bear*

with a mind to see one in the willows.
Though the creek is mostly ankle-shallow,

this small oxbow looks deep

enough to swim. With no one near,
why not ask for rebirth

and enter as a jay, cleanly

in its crystal chatter? It would be ice
if not for gravity calling melt

down from the peaks. Water so cold it burns.

So cold it burns clean through your body
and what is left but the bright zing

of something tender for the sun.

Here, you can air-dry in a lasso of light,
then dress and sit on a hummock

with an apple, dreaming of your past

life, riding a particle wake downstream,
back in the direction from which you came.

REPEAT AFTER ME

It is good to be strange
& if you are lucky you will

not linger in the mirror
but find yourself in song

casting about an imagined
pond for what shimmers

back   the body always
on its way out of the frame

out of the golden glow
endemic to a phase of youth

Think of the light as it summers
through a flock of leaves

willow or cottonwood
Isn't it more beautiful then

in that scattered mercurial
installment brightening the dirt

THE LISTENER

And when she spoke, the rain was mesh against late sun,

the lightest of veils woven over the outside world as she was

backlit and mostly silhouetted, a rain nearly weightless,

a screen to deepen to the field below the wooded hills,

so that her words were merely the sound of this movement,

and I placed both feet solidly on the ground and set my shoulders

back, filling my chest with the space of listening,

holding my gaze at the collaboration, also a part of the making

of this fabric, by making room, being willing to suspend

my smallness, my isolation lie, and join in among the strands,

taking care to affirm the thread, an end in each hand,

to become one with the work of keeping things together.

GHAZAL OF LOST YEARS

Out of the dream, we made two sons and learned that love was letting go,
a life made up of days, of longer hours, somehow letting minutes go

to ache for sleep or the chance to read a book or meet a friend to talk
about what was most alive in the middle years, letting go

of our dreams, somehow looking back upon a sheaf of pages scattering in the wind,
hurts often brighter than the joys, especially for us who numbed the years, letting go

of first steps and picture books, who cooed lullabies to our young, thick-tongued,
slurring love in a musk of booze, for us who seemed to think that letting go

meant being stoned, meant not remembering in the dawn, and so, somehow, years
just disappeared, and that was a part of how we learned what love was not. *Let go,*

I sing each night before the mirror. Mateo, love is showing up so fully it hurts.
You couldn't have known this from the start. The past cannot be owned.

FOR WHAT IT'S WORTH

I'd repeat my sons exactly
as they are, even the one

with the now blue hair still asleep
at the foot of my bed. I'd repeat

the night I met my wife and even
the middle years of purgatorial sorrow.

Three times, at least, I'd repeat last
night's sunset, of which I could see

a framed square of downy furrows
deepening from rose to bruise

while I sat in the filling tub, book
in hand, already partway out

of this world. Though it would not
bring me any joy at all, I would

repeat three times the day I did not
pull the trigger, or the day I almost

pushed the sharpest knife
we owned between my ribs.

Three times, at least, I would
enter the water, walking toward

the sun, the water needle-cold,
all of it, in its own way, surging

toward an epic repetition—
I may be on the other side

of some things, but I have not
yet seen the longest night.

HOW TO LOVE THE UNFINISHED DREAM

There it is again—that
little *pop* of possibility

sparking in my brain.
It's an effervescent joy

I can map out fully
in my mind from blue-

prints to the manual.
I have all the tools

even & the know-how.
O, what a bit of bare sky

& sun will do
to a winter mood.

It is the purest heaven—
& the only kind

I believe in: brief
& ending the very moment

awareness mounts
the stone staircase

of the mind. It was
good though, wasn't it?

That little bite of bread
after so long without—

SOMEDAY, IF I AM LUCKY

I will be survived by this open acre

ringed by cedars and firs, this

meadow collecting yellow light,

where today, alive, I linger

in the listening, housed in a shape

capable of such ordinary song. I wish

to thank the minerals in my bones

and all this borrowed epiphany, all this

endless ache linking arms with sorrow.

May many tomorrows nest

in such green valleys. May we all

accept the ground we will become.

GHAZAL OF AIR

When will it happen? That we will finally see castles in air
and know how to traverse the distance like motes meant for air?

Will it be this life in which we finally destroy our home?
What hate we have pastured, slipping our knives into the fabric of air.

Will it be as my six-year-old son has foretold? That his generation
will be the last of all people? His prophecy emptied the air

from my satchel and turned over the artifact of our name.
Without understanding the logic, he moves between worlds in air.

He sees what I fail to see and says without fear what may come to pass.
A small body for such an engine of thought, I can still toss him high in the air

and catch him in laughter, but those days are almost gone. He still calls me *Papa*
in the language of skin. I ask my grandfather to hold me. I speak to the air.

MULTITUDES

A hymn is what time does with the body.
The singing isn't for us but we can listen in.

Out of the One we enter and splinter into
the ego's *I* and endure, detached, eras of solos

and deem this right, the way of the world
we inhabit. But listen (and I don't mean

to the words, but what is under the words
and beyond the sound): the world inhabits us,

gives flesh to the idea of bone, makes
a space inside the shape of a body which

is to remain empty and, therefore, true—
the world does not belong to us even as we

contain what makes the world. At thirty,
I had tattooed on my wrist Whitman's apology

to himself, the one that speaks of contradictions—
and for a couple years, the letters of the smallish font

held out as crisp individuals I could pass my fingers
over—*m u l t i t u d e s*—a dream house

of a body, and one in which to dream without
worry of being wrong, and so, like Whitman, I sang

of it, but mostly with a sadness for years of being sorry
for being. The body likes the song and relaxes

into the listening, if one is lucky. O, failure,
my greatest teacher, I bow before you even as you

kick sand into my face. I'm to remain at your feet
as the letters wash into themselves, as the words

become unreadable, and only then, perhaps,
briefly understood. The body goes. It was nothing personal.

JUST ACROSS THE WHEEL FROM YOU

All winter, I sent letters to old friends turned strangers,
ghosts, representations of other eras, statues & facades.

I spoke of sobriety & struggle. I spoke of fatherhood
& a new masculine energy tended in the intimacy of a circle

of other initiated men. Who am I trying to impress?
My teenage son calls everybody bro, even me. He tells me

to STFU & still wants me to rub his feet before bed. I want
to open him like a matryoshka doll & let the little River breathe—

that tender, kind boy I never see anymore. I want to hold
his hand as we walk through the park, his stuffed animal kitty

dragging tail through wet grass toward the swings. I don't write
any of this in the letters, though maybe I should. Maybe

such details are worth more than all the *xs* & *os*, the postcards
& envelopes coursing slowly across the continent. I am an envelope

of anxiety, pulsing purple thistle, spiny & purposeful. Make meaning
of that, America. Every legend I know ends with a lesson in loss.

AND THEN

I took off my shame

like a dress

made of light.

Like a dress

made of the self-

spun cocoon.

I was not beautiful.

It was not about beauty.

Beneath my shame,

the body

was a raw, red thing,

untrained in acceptance.

But the air was delicate

and cool as a mother

blowing gently

on a burn.

I had lived so long

in the fabric,

I thought it my skin.

I had forgotten

how new

anyone forgiven

can become.

ACKNOWLEDGMENTS

Many thanks to the editors of the publications where some of these poems first appeared, sometimes in slightly different forms.

32 Poems:	"Early Onset"
Alaska Quarterly Review:	"On the Condition of Being Born"
Beloit Poetry Journal:	"Every Gift Carries a Cost"
Bennington Review:	"After the Fire"
Copper Nickel:	"Useless Prayer" "It Could Be That My Heart Was Not in It"
The Cortland Review:	"They Once Looked to Me"
Diode:	"Seams of Starlight & Flecks of Gold" "An Echo for the Archives"

The Georgia Review:	"Letter of Recommendation"
	"Bookending the Day"
	"The Listener"
	"Ghazal of Air"
Gulf Coast:	"What Luck"
The Los Angeles Review:	"I Almost Forget"
Missouri Review:	"And Then"
New England Review:	"Multitudes"
North American Review:	"At Midlife Trying to Recall My Twenties"
Only Poems:	"Apologia"
	"Cocoon"
	"For What It's Worth"
	"Four Years to the Day"
	"How to Love the Unfinished Dream"
	"The Return"
Ploughshares:	"Just Across the Wheel from You"
Sewanee Review:	"History"
	"Someday, If I Am Lucky"
Southern Humanities Review:	"Ownership"
Terrain.org:	"Dusk Loop"
	"Ghazal of Lost Years"
	"In All the Wrong Places"
	"No Painting Worth Its Paint"
	"Ode to ADD"
Tupelo Quarterly:	"Begin Again"
	"Even If the Past Is Not a Place You Can Visit"

| *Waxwing*: | "My Disorder" |

| *wildness*: | "If You Think You Know the Way" |
| | "Repeat after Me" |

| *Willow Springs*: | "Getting off Antidepressants" |

"Letter of Recommendation" was featured on Spokane Public Radio on June 16, 2021, selected and read by Derek Sheffield.

"The Listener" and "On the Condition of Being Born" were featured on the *Lay Me Down* podcast (Episodes 1 & 2, Season 2).

————————————

Though I walked and worked alone for far too long, lonely and filled with shame, the long, slow arc of making this book over several years was supported in many ways by my partner, Elie, and our two sons.

Somehow, out of and through the darkness, Ash Bowen and I began a daily correspondence in which some of these poems were first shared. For his friendship and encouragement, I am ever grateful.

Rikki Ducornet was the first and only reader of the book as a whole before I sent it off to Alice James. Without her encouragement, it may have never left my desk.

To Carey Salerno, I am tremendously thankful for your close readings, your generosity, and your trust. To Emily Marquis, Alyssa Neptune, Lacey Dunham, and Genevieve Hartman, I know this book would not be an object in the world without your gifts and energy.

To Morgan LaRocca and the *Poets & Writers* 2024 Get the Word Out cohort, thank you for helping me grow my ability to know my work more deeply so that I might share it more clearly with the world.

Kaveh Akbar, Eduardo C. Corral, Tomás Q. Morín, and Corey Van Landingham! I can't thank you enough for spending time with these poems and lending your voices here. It is a gift I will not forget.

Derek and Rafa—thank you for walking alongside me as I began to find my way toward purpose, honesty, and true accountability. Ditto to all the other men I know who are showing up and doing the deeper work.

To my sons, River and Paikea, thank you for inspiring me and leading the way toward health. To my parents, abundant gratitude for your never-ending love, support, and generosity. And to Elie, again and again, for love, forgiveness, challenge, and support—I am so lucky to be your partner.

And finally, to all my teachers and friends in writing—even if we haven't spoken in years, or if there is some mending required to move forward—you are a part of what continues to make this work possible.

RECENT TITLES FROM ALICE JAMES BOOKS

Alice James Books is committed to publishing books that matter. The press was founded in 1973 in Boston, Massachusetts to give women access to publishing. As a cooperative, authors performed the day-to-day undertakings of the press. The press continues to expand and grow from its formative roots, guided by its founding values of access, excellence, inclusivity, and collaboration in publishing. Its mission is to publish books that matter and preserve a place of belonging for poets who inspire us. AJB seeks to broaden our collective interpretation of what constitutes the American poetic voice and is dedicated to helping its artists achieve purposeful engagement with broad audiences and communities nationwide. The press was named for Alice James, sister to William and Henry, whose extraordinary gift for writing went unrecognized during her lifetime.

Designed by Tiani Kennedy

Printed by Versa Press